Losing Someone You Love
Dealing With Death and Dying

Losing Someone You Love
Dealing With Death and Dying

ISSUES IN FOCUS TODAY

Tracy A. Phillips

Enslow Publishers, Inc.
40 Industrial Road
Box 398
Berkeley Heights, NJ 07922
USA

http://www.enslow.com

Library of Congress Cataloging-in-Publication Data

Phillips, Tracy.
    Losing someone you love : dealing with death and dying / Tracy A. Phillips.
       p. cm. — (Issues in focus today)
    Includes bibliographical references and index.
    Summary: "Discusses the loss of a loved one and coping with death and dying, including the grieving process, developing a support system, and children and teens learning to deal with loss"—Provided by publisher.
    ISBN-13: 978-0-7660-3067-1
    ISBN-10: 0-7660-3067-9
    1. Death—Psychological aspects—Juvenile literature. 2. Bereavement—Psychological aspects—Juvenile literature. 3. Death. 4. Grief. I. Title.
    BF789.D4P49 2009
    155.9'37—dc22

                          2008042872

Printed in the United States of America

10 9 8 7 6 5 4 3 2 1

Illustration Credits: All photos are from Shutterstock except for the following: AP/Wide World, pp. 15, 23, 74, 77, 87; iStockphoto.com, p. 85.

Cover Illustration: Shutterstock (large photo); BananaStock (small inset photo).

Contents

Death Is a Part of Life

Julie Smith was just seventeen when she learned of the sudden death of her very good friend Kevin. He too was just seventeen and had died suddenly from complications of juvenile diabetes. He had just been accepted on a scholarship to a well-known college where he planned on studying medicine so he could help young people, much like the doctors and nurses he had dealt with over the years who had helped him. Everyone liked him because of his sense of humor.

For Julie, the news of Kevin's death seemed impossible. This must be some kind of sick joke, she thought. Who would joke about something like this? She soon got angry at the thought that someone would make a joke of this. It then hit her: This was not a joke; he was gone. She knew his diabetes was serious, but never in her wildest dreams had she imagined that her good friend would die.

This was the first death Julie had really experienced. Her grandparents were gone before she was old enough to know them. About a year before Kevin died, he and Julie had a falling out, as teenage friends often do, and they did not speak to each other for a period of time. However, a few months before his death, Kevin called Julie, and they reconciled. Julie was grateful that they had that time together before he died. It would have been more difficult for her to deal with the loss had they still not been speaking. She coped with grief in her own way. She "cried a lot, stayed alone a lot, and watched old family videos he was in," she said.[1] She feels that each person grieves in his or her own way. "Everyone deals with things differently; you're the only person that knows how to handle your feelings."[2]

It has been ten years since Kevin's death, and Julie still gets sad when she thinks about the loss of her friend. "It still upsets me; I still go to his grave and check on his family," she said.[3] Julie's advice to someone going through the emotional loss of a friend or loved one: "Try not to dwell on the past; the person wouldn't want you to stay sad forever."[4]

What Is Grief?

Grief is a natural response to loss. As humans, we grieve the loss of a loved one, the loss of a friend, the loss of a pet, the loss of a job, the loss of a cherished possession, and even the loss of a game. Each person experiences grief in a unique way. However, there are responses that are common to many people grieving the loss of a loved one. These responses are an indication of the emotional states that many grieving people go through at some point during their sadness. It can be helpful for teens to have knowledge of the emotions related to grief when trying to help others or trying to cope with a loss themselves.

The grieving process can affect a person physically as well as emotionally. It is common for a person who is grieving to have changes in sleep patterns, appetite, and even personality. In particular, younger people experiencing grief for the first time may feel as though this loss is actually happening to someone else, as if it is not real.[5] These strong emotions can be overwhelming.

The loss of someone close is difficult regardless of a person's age. However, teens are especially vulnerable to emotional turmoil when dealing with the loss of a loved one. Teens may not have been exposed to death before, and as a result, some may feel a sense of indestructibility, as if nothing can stop them or hurt them. Teens may have assumed that their friend or family member would always be there for them. If that person dies, the shock and grief can be devastating. It is important for the people in a grieving teen's life to continue to keep the lines of communication open and to be there for him or her, to talk about these new feelings if he or she is ready to talk. A grieving teen should never have to feel isolated.

> Each person experiences grief in a unique way. However, there are responses that are common to many people grieving the loss of a loved one.

What People Can Do

It can be a bit awkward to spend time with someone who is grieving, as it is often hard to know what to say. People may feel helpless in the situation. However, just being there for someone, offering support, can be extremely helpful.

One of the most important things that someone can do for a grieving friend or family member is to offer to listen. Letting a person talk about the loss can help. If the grieving person wants it, activities such as going to the mall or playing video games can help take his or her mind off of things.

Grief is a natural response to loss. Especially for young people experiencing serious loss for the first time, the strong emotions can be overwhelming.

It is important that people do not distance themselves from grieving teens or treat them differently. Although change is going on in their lives, they need some things that are constant. Being treated differently by a friend or family member may make them feel like an outcast and contribute to their grief.

Life-Changing Experiences

Humans have strong emotional connections to each other and strong relationships with one another. The loss of a loved one or friend can cause a void in a person's life—a void that may never be filled. Each person has a unique relationship with each person they hold close, and people act differently in different relationships. One person may be a responsible daughter to her parents but a fun-loving and carefree companion to her best friend. When there is a loss of that relationship due to death or illness, people may suffer depression or a sense of hopelessness because someone they identified with, someone who was a part of them, is now gone. Now there is emptiness, a loss of a part of themselves, in a sense.

Getting On With Life

There is a lot going on in the days and weeks after a death. Often the house is full of people. Friends bring food, stop by to offer condolences, check in to see how the family of the deceased is doing. There are arrangements to be made for a funeral or memorial service. Sometimes these distractions help those who are grieving. They have something to focus their attention on. It is when all of this stops—the funeral is over, the neighbors do not stop by as often to check in—that it becomes quiet. For some grieving people, this may be the first time the loss truly hits them.

It is important for those who are grieving to understand that these feelings of emptiness are not uncommon. If a loved one is gone, it is okay to feel a loss. To not feel a loss might indicate

It's important for the people in a grieving teen's life to keep the lines of communication open.

A Poet on Loss

"The Widower" was a poem written by Rudyard Kipling. It demonstrates the unending love between a husband and wife, even in the presence of death.

For a season there must be pain—
For a little, little space
I shall lose the sight of her face,
Take back the old life again
While she is at rest in her place.

For a season this pain must endure,
For a little, little while
I shall sigh more often than smile
Till Time shall work me a cure,
And the pitiful days beguile.

For that season we must be apart,
For a little length of years,
Till my life's last hour nears,
And, above the beat of my heart,
I hear Her voice in my ears.

But I shall not understand—
Being set on some later love,
Shall not know her for whom I strove,
Till she reach me forth her hand,
Saying, "Who but I have the right?"
And out of a troubled night
Shall draw me safe to the land.

that the person is ignoring his or her feelings and not properly grieving.[6] Sometimes people try to ignore what they don't understand or what scares them.

Some people try to block out memories of the person who is now gone, as thinking of him or her is too painful. Conversely, other people become obsessed with the loss, tending to stay focused on the past rather than on the present or future. Some people feel guilty. They may think of times that they were not as kind as they feel they should have been to the person who is now gone. It is nearly impossible to have a close and strong relationship with a person and not have at least a few regrets about something said or done.

If Only . . .

Sometimes the guilt over past actions is painful. A person might think, "If only I had told him I loved him," or "If only I had walked home with him, he would not have been in that car accident and would be alive today." It is not healthy to stay focused on those types of thoughts, as the *if only*s will only create more despair. It is impossible to change the past, and staying focused on the past takes away from focusing on the present and getting through each day. It is important to focus on the positive parts of the relationship and the happy memories. All people make mistakes. Every close relationship has its good times and its bad times. It is important not to focus on the bad times.

Each relationship has its place in a person's life. People have different kinds of bonds with grandparents than with their parents, for example. When a death alters that relationship, other issues may arise that the grieving person did not foresee. For example, the loss of a parent brings feelings of sadness but also feelings of insecurity. Children may feel frightened for the future, as one of their primary caregivers is now gone. They may have fear that the surviving parent will die as well and that then they will be an orphan. When a husband loses a wife, he may feel that his partner in life is gone, and he may fear going through life alone and sad, wondering if he will ever be truly happy again.

Each loss carries with it unique feelings and emotions. The loss of a pet can be devastating. After all, pets can be humans'

In a candlelight vigil, community members in Wisconsin gather to mourn the death of a murdered man. Rituals can help ease the grief for many people.

best friends. However, the feelings of sadness may not be the same type of sadness that people experience when they lose their parent or grandparent. For each unique personal relationship people have as family members, there are unique issues surrounding that loss. In this book, each chapter will explore the unique relationships teens have with their friends, family members, and pets, and the emotional ties involved in each relationship. This book's purpose is to provide a better understanding of these issues so that people will be able to offer support and guidance to grieving friends and family and will know where to look for help with their own grief. This book explores the support options that are available to teens and the need for counseling and support from peers going through a similar situation. It will cover the signs of grief and how to know when teens may be in need of professional help to deal with their grief issues.

The Grieving Process

Learning about the grieving process is helpful to individuals coping with a loss, because it helps them understand normal human reactions to a difficult situation. Many researchers have spent years studying the human reaction to death and have offered theories for how people cope with grief. Some theories conflict, while other theories build upon ideas from the past.

One cannot discuss the grieving process without mentioning Elisabeth Kübler-Ross, a psychiatrist who developed five stages to describe the ways in which people deal with death. Initially, Kübler-Ross's research dealt with dying people and their reactions to the realization of their impending death.

These stages were eventually applied to all areas of bereavement. Although these stages of grief have been criticized by some as being too rigid, they are used by many professionals in the mental health field to help people cope with loss.

Kübler-Ross's model has been widely criticized for being too broad. Not everyone will go through every stage, and some people may even go back to a previous stage. J. William Worden, Ph.D., a well-known grief therapist, finds that setting forth stages may result in people taking the stages too literally, thinking that everyone must go through each stage in some neat order.[1]

Kübler-Ross's Stages

Elisabeth Kübler-Ross's stages consist of the following steps: denial, anger, bargaining, depression, and acceptance.

Denial. Denial is a defense mechanism. It is a way of either consciously or unconsciously refusing to accept certain facts. When told of devastating news, a person may initially react with disbelief, insisting that the person who gave the news must be mistaken. This is the mind's way of initially rejecting information that may be too painful to accept at that time. When a person comes out of the denial phase, the reality of the situation can be devastating. He or she is left with having to figure out a way to deal with the intense emotions of sadness and despair.

Anger. Once people come to grips with the reality of a situation, like the death of a loved one, they often get angry. This anger may be directed at God, at a person who could be responsible for their grief, or at anyone available to assign with blame. Sometimes people are even angry with the person who died. Why didn't he wear his seat belt? Why did she have to smoke when she knew she could get cancer? Anger is a normal response to a difficult situation.[2] But it is important to deal with anger in a healthy manner.

For example, the parents of a murdered child suffer through

grief that most people cannot understand. The anger associated with such a senseless and brutal murder can destroy lives. Some grieving parents attempt to channel their anger into something that will help others. One example is the case of Megan Kanka. On July 29, 1994, Megan Kanka was a beautiful, happy seven-year-old girl living in the suburbs of New Jersey with her family. On that day, she was lured out of her house by a neighbor who lived across the street. He had promised to show her a puppy. Megan was sexually assaulted, brutally murdered, and dumped in a nearby park.

The killer, Jesse Timmendequas, was a convicted sex offender. However, people in the neighborhood did not know his history. At the time, the law did not allow police departments to notify the public of a sex offender's past. Had people in Megan Kanka's community known that Timmendequas was a sex offender, Megan might be alive today.

Timmendequas was found guilty of Megan's murder and sentenced to death. Years after he was sentenced, New Jersey abolished the death penalty, and Timmendequas's sentence was reduced to life in prison without the possibility of parole.[3]

> Kübler-Ross's stages of grief have been criticized by some as being too rigid, but they are used by many mental health professionals to help people cope with loss.

Richard and Maureen Kanka, Megan's parents, made it their mission to fight to allow the disclosure of sex offender status throughout the country. They took the anger they were feeling regarding the murder of their daughter and turned it into energy to fight for something they believed would save lives. As a result of their efforts, Megan's Law was born. Now every state must have a process in place for notifying concerned residents of sex offenders living within their community.

Bargaining. The next stage that Kübler-Ross identified was the bargaining stage. This stage is often seen in cases of terminal illness, in which the dying person or his or her loved ones bargain, or negotiate, for a different outcome. Often this bargaining is with God or a higher power of some sort. Some people make promises: "If you only save her, I will be a better person," or "I will give to charity."

Forty years ago, Mary Kukovich was just fourteen when her mother died of brain cancer at the age of forty-one. She said:

> I did [bargain] before she died, particularly the summer she was dying. I remember trying to tell God that it would make more sense for Him to take me (though, in candor, I secretly hoped he would spare us both). I was upset with the unfairness of it all: This was a woman who was incredibly devoted to God and who was loved by many. The night before she died, I remember being especially upset and unable to sleep; I was up most of the night. I finally fell asleep on our sun porch just before dawn with the most amazing sense of calm and peacefulness. Not long after that, my dad woke me up to say she had died. I think she waited to die until I could come to terms with it.[4]

Depression. When it becomes clear that bargaining has failed, depression can set in. A feeling of unanswered calls for help from God and the universe can create a feeling of despair along with such thoughts as, "What is the point? I just don't care anymore." People can experience depression by which both the physical and emotional aspects of their lives can be altered, having feelings of immense sadness along with disturbances in sleep patterns, eating habits, and concentration.

The National Health Information Center distinguishes depression from grief, stating that clinical depression is a whole-body disorder that can take over the way people think and feel. According to a list on the center's Web site, depression can have the following symptoms:

- a sad, anxious, or empty mood that won't go away
- loss of interest in what you used to enjoy
- low energy, fatigue, or feeling slowed down

People react to loss in their own way. Common reactions include denial, anger, and depression.

- changes in sleep patterns
- loss of appetite, weight loss, or weight gain
- trouble concentrating, remembering, or making decisions
- feeling hopeless or gloomy
- feeling guilty, worthless, or helpless
- thoughts of death or suicide or a suicide attempt
- recurring aches and pains that do not respond to treatment[5]

It is important for loved ones and friends to be aware of situations in which someone's sadness about the death of a loved one turns into depression. The person may be in need of professional help.

Acceptance. Reaching this stage does not mean that one is necessarily happy. Once it becomes clear that the bargaining has not worked and a new reality has emerged, people understand that they cannot change this situation and they must learn to cope with it in the best way possible. For those who have lost a loved one, this is the time when denial is no longer present and the stark reality emerges—that life will have to go on without this loved one.

Mary Kukovich said:

> I'm not sure that *accepting it* is the right term for me. I have always believed in a life after death, though not necessarily embracing the same faith as my parents. While losing Mom was incredibly sad, I also felt she was no longer in pain . . . and she certainly believed in and was comforted by her belief in a life after death. Our parents' religious faith was a real force in their marriage, and it was a model for us in dealing with Mom's death. Our dad really led us through his actions. There was no doubt that there was tremendous and powerful love between them, and that he missed her terribly, but he never made us feel neglected or less important in his life after she died.
>
> One of the powerful things they did together before she died was plan for a celebration, not a funeral, which at the time was a pretty radical thing. She didn't want people standing around crying and mourning her loss; she wanted us to celebrate her new life. So instead of a quiet wake after the funeral, we had a wonderful picnic at our house. That was a very strong message.[6]

Building on Existing Ideas

Two psychiatrists, John Bowlby and Colin Murray Parkes, wanting to improve upon Kübler-Ross's ideas of a grief process, created their own four-phase model of grief. It focused on the attachments people have with others in their life. Some of the emotions in their stages overlap with some of the ideas of Kübler-Ross's model.

Pallbearers carry the casket of a student killed at Columbine High School. Just after a death, many people have feelings of shock and numbness.

Numbness. In the first phase, people who experience a loss are shocked and numb. They understand what has happened, but it has not become a reality to them. They are in a state of disbelief. They may make decisions, arrange for the funeral, and talk to loved ones, all the while feeling as if they are in a daze or even a dream state. It is the mind's way of protecting itself against reality. The reality will hit them in time, but right now, they are protecting themselves. This allows the person to still be able to function even in the worst circumstances.

Yearning. In the second phase, the reality has started to sink in. Here people struggle with intense emotions. They may experience anger and guilt and think of all the possible *if onlys*, but mostly they just long for the person who has died. They may see their loved one in their dreams and think they hear his or her voice. They want more than anything to turn back time and make this situation right and to stop feeling this overwhelming grief and pain. They cannot visualize a world without the person who is now gone.

Disorganization and despair. In the third phase, it becomes clear that the deceased person is not coming back. As a result, the people grieving may feel despair, depression, and apathy toward life. They may have a hard time returning to everyday life and, as a result, have a hard time managing responsibilities in their lives.

Reorganization. When grieving people reach this stage, they have accepted the loss. Their life may never be the same, but they are able to go on living. The intense feelings of grief will occur less frequently, and the apathy they were feeling toward life will subside. In this phase, grieving people will make an effort to connect with those who are still living.

Tasks

J. William Worden, who took issue with grief stages, claims that while adapting to their new life without their loved one, people must complete a set of tasks in order to complete mourning.[7] The completion of these tasks does not necessarily have to be done in this order.

Task I: To accept the reality of the loss. As mentioned in Parkes and Bowlby's research, there is a sense of disbelief when someone has died. In this task, grieving people must accept the fact that their loved one is gone and is not coming back. Here they may experience dreams of the deceased person or may even think they catch a glimpse of him or her in a restaurant or on a bus. To work through this task, grieving people must get through any denial and understand that their loved one is gone.

Corinne Hanson lost her husband to cancer in 2004. For her, sending in the appropriate documentation for her husband's life insurance policy benefits was a difficult thing to do. She said, "I felt funny about filing the claim—as if he might come back if I never mailed the letter."[8]

Task II: To work through the pain of the grief. Grieving people need to face the feelings associated with grief. These may be feelings of sadness, anger, anxiety, guilt, or loneliness. Whatever the feelings are, they should not be suppressed or avoided, because they may show up later on in life if they are not worked through.[9] Many grieving people are just not prepared to face the intensity of the emotions that occur during grief, and it can be a natural response to try to avoid them.

People in the early stages of grief may make decisions, arrange for the funeral, and talk to loved ones, all the while feeling as if they are in a daze.

Task III: To adjust to an environment in which the deceased is missing. Worden speaks of three types of adjustments that people need to make after they have lost a loved one: external, internal, and spiritual. External adjustments include getting used to everyday life without the deceased person. Internal adjustments describe how grieving people feel now that their loved one is gone. During this adjustment, there is a focus on how the loss has affected their sense of self. Lastly, spiritual adjustments include how the grieving person now sees the world and their belief system.

Task IV: To emotionally relocate the deceased and move on with life. This task may prove to be the most difficult for people who are grieving.[10] Here grieving people need to allow themselves to love again. Their life cannot stop when their loved one dies. They need to go on. They need to live with the memories of that person—but they need to live, nonetheless.

Worden differentiates his list of tasks from stages, pointing out that in his model, each task can be revisited and reworked over time. People can go through them differently and at different times. This allows people to feel that they can grieve at their own pace and in their own way.

Complicated Grief

Some researchers have been taking a new approach to grief. Focusing on companionship rather than treatment, Alan D. Wolfelt, Ph.D., addresses the importance of being emotionally available for a person in mourning. In his book *Understanding Grief: Helping Yourself Heal*, he discusses how it is more helpful to be there as support for a person rather than being there to treat the person. He also distinguishes normal grief from complicated grief. Complicated grief issues include:

True depression goes beyond a feeling of sadness. It can include a loss of interest in normal activities, low energy, trouble concentrating, and recurring aches and pains.

- **Postponing grief**: Delaying expression of grief indefinitely
- **Displacing grief**: Directing feelings of grief to other parts of one's life
- **Replacing grief**: Investing feelings in another relationship in an effort to avoid grieving
- **Minimizing grief**: Using rationalization to minimize feelings of grief
- **Somatizing grief**: Converting feelings of grief into physical symptoms[11]

Each of these, according to Wolfelt, is a way for people to avoid the feelings associated with grief and can be a sign of complicated grief, which may require the help of a professional grief therapist.

Recent Findings

A recent study aimed to examine the stage theory popularized by Kübler-Ross. The Yale Bereavement Study was conducted over a three-year period and included 233 people who had suffered a loss from a natural death, such as disease or illness, and not a traumatic death, such as an accident or a suicide. Each participant was interviewed three times over two years. The study measured stages of grief—disbelief, yearning, anger, depression, and acceptance—according to how frequently and at what point after the loss these feelings occurred. The study found that depression is not an inevitable response to loss, as was commonly thought. Rather, yearning was the most common reaction. Holly Prigerson, Ph.D., one of the authors of the study, said, "Up to now, people thought sadness was the most characteristic feature of bereavement, but these data show it is more about yearning and pining and missing the person—a hunger for having them come back."[12] The study also found that on average, negative symptoms peaked at six months and were on the decline after that point.

The finding that negative emotions reached their peak at six months suggests that people suffering from more prolonged symptoms may be in need of professional help at that point. Prigerson said:

> People never get over a loss, they just get used to it. Even years after someone died, they get pangs of grief, they need to think about the person and they miss them with heartache. That's normal. But intense levels beyond that become problematic.[13]

Grief in Younger People

Researchers are conflicted about the ways in which children mourn. Can infants mourn the loss of a parent if they cannot comprehend death? This question is often debated by grief experts in the field, and no true consensus has been reached. However, most would agree that children have to have a mental image of the loved one and must also be aware of their constant presence in their life to really mourn that person.[14] This level of understanding is usually present around three to four years of age.[15]

Worden, who developed the tasks associated with grief, states that children's emotional, cognitive, and social development must be considered when looking at a child's mourning process. He holds that his task theory can be applied to children, but that depending on their level of understanding, they may have difficulty with some of the tasks. If a child is not able to understand finality, he or she may have a hard time with the first task of accepting the reality of the loss. Worden admits that while he feels the tasks can be applied to younger children, some children may struggle with these tasks, depending on their level of functioning.[16]

Developmental level has an effect on a child's ability to understand loss. Some children display what is known as magical thinking—a type of nonscientific reasoning that includes such ideas as connections between unrelated events

The way children react to death is related to their emotional, cognitive, and social development.

and the mind's ability to affect the physical world. For instance, children may believe that somehow they have caused the death and feel guilty as a result. Some children are worried that they will die soon, too. The emotions that affect children are more complicated because of their level of understanding of death and their surroundings in general. They may not be able to fully comprehend the loss and, as a result, may not experience many of the emotions of grief that an adult might.

Teenagers are much more advanced cognitively than younger children. As a result, they will grieve much like adults do.[17] However, unlike adults who must handle their grief while dealing with adult responsibilities, teenagers must deal with their grief while facing the pressures of adolescence. It is an emotional time for them, one of constant change and peer pressure. Dealing with the loss of a loved one during this time can make teens especially vulnerable to emotions they have never experienced before.

Researchers may disagree with each other regarding which emotion is felt most strongly during the grieving process and how adults and children handle grief. However, the psychiatric community agrees on one thing: Grieving people are going to go through an array of emotions, and those emotions will affect them for a long time.

Losing a Parent

Maureen O'Brien Smith, now forty-nine, lost her mother when she was nine. Her mother was forty-one at the time. This loss has affected her throughout her life. "I do regret that I don't remember her more," she said. "My memories of her are so vague, just pictures in my head. I do wish I could know more about her, as I find her life so incredible."[1] O'Brien Smith stated that she was in disbelief at first, but "it hits you quick when they are no longer there on a day-to-day basis. I don't ever remember being told my mom was going to die. I knew she was very ill but never realized she would be gone."[2]

A child comes into this world completely dependent on his

or her parents for everything—food, shelter, and love. Children often think the world of their parents. For many children, no person on earth can match their mom or dad. For many parents, the love for a child is unconditional. Parents will love their children regardless of how they look or behave.

When children lose a parent, it can feel as if the world as they know it has come crashing down upon them. The familiar place they may have known as home has disappeared, and what is left is sadness and uncertainty—uncertainty about what will happen now and who will take care of them. Even after the initial shock and sorrow subside, there will be difficult days ahead. Children soon realize that for those milestones of life—birthdays, graduations, weddings—their parent will not be there. These very joyous occasions will never be entirely happy, as there will always be a missing piece—the parent who has died. Children can often wonder, "Why me?" They may question why this tragedy has happened to them and may feel that life is not fair.

The Surviving Parent

When a parent dies, often the surviving parent is left to keep everything together. He or she too is grieving, but there are still responsibilities. The surviving parent may mourn often when it is quiet and no one else is around. He or she may be lonely and have anxiety about the future. The parent who is left, or the guardian who is now tasked with caring for young children, must take on this two-person job alone. Grieving while caring for a family and home can be a challenge. A household that may have had two people contributing to it now only has one.

The shift in the household responsibilities can create additional anxieties for the parent or guardian and the children. At some point, maybe a month or two after the funeral services, it might be helpful for the parent and children to discuss the shift in duties in the household in a family meeting in which teamwork and cooperation are emphasized.[3] The family can now work as a team to try to deal with their new family dynamic.

Some parents decide after time has elapsed that they want a new partner to share their life with. Many people remarry after their spouse has died. If there are children involved, even adult children, this can sometimes cause turmoil within the family. It can be further complicated if the new partner also has children, too, because the families may now merge and live together.

Stepfamilies

Acquiring a stepfamily can be a stressful process. Children have not chosen this family. In some cases, they have not even been consulted on this decision. In their mind, the situation may feel forced. There may be feelings that the surviving parent is betraying the memory of the deceased parent. If children accept this new person, they may feel as if they are betraying the deceased parent. This is not an uncommon reaction for young children, teens, and even adult children in this type of situation. Children who have lost a parent usually do not want someone to

When children lose a parent, it can feel as if the world as they know it has come crashing down on them.

replace that parent. There is usually a special place for that parent that can never be filled, and if the child feels that someone is trying to take the dead parent's place, conflict can arise.

It can be helpful for parents to discuss the issue of remarriage or moving in together before it actually happens to give children time to let this information sink in and to ensure that they do not feel blindsided.

In Maureen O'Brien Smith's case, her father did remarry. Her new stepmother suddenly had five children, ranging in age from ten to sixteen years old. O'Brien Smith now feels that counseling would have been helpful, because a parent's remarriage is a big adjustment for children—especially teenagers. She recommends having the whole family discuss the issue of remarriage before any decisions are made, and if the children have concerns, the family should seek counseling.[4]

Helping a Grieving Teen

Since the bond between a parent and child is so strong, when a teen loses a parent, everyone left in the family needs to look out for that teen and provide emotional support. One goal might be to provide support so that teens do not have to look for unhealthy ways to deal with their feelings, such as drugs or alcohol. There is enough confusion in the teenage years without a major loss. Add to it the death of a parent, and this could be the mixture for self-destruction. Even though other family members

When a parent dies, the surviving parent has the difficult double job of dealing with his or her own grief and helping the children in the family with theirs.

are dealing with their own grief, they need to look out for teens during this time.

It is important for surviving parents to try to keep things as normal as possible. If Friday night is movie night, for instance, that tradition should be continued. Teens may feel guilty about continuing with movie night when one parent has died. They may feel guilty for having fun and may believe that the deceased parent would think that he or she is not missed. But teens need to understand that most parents would want them to be happy and not to mourn indefinitely. It is important that teens realize that it is okay to go on with life and enjoy themselves again.

Everyone needs to feel that the way he or she has chosen to grieve is okay, because each person grieves in his or her own unique way. Some children feel that they want to talk about the deceased parent. For others, it is too painful and they choose not to speak of the person, at least not right away. Any way that they are coping, so long as it is not destructive and harmful to themselves or others, should be respected.

Sometimes children worry that they will forget the parent who has died. Unlike the surviving parent, the child may not have had as many years with that person, and memories may fade. If a child wants to talk about the deceased parent, this should be fostered by the rest of the family, as talking about that person will keep the memories alive for the child.

Issues in Adulthood

Like others who have experienced a loss, most people who lose a parent never fully get over it but merely learn to live with it. It becomes a part of who they are. Barbara Smith, cousin of Maureen O'Brien Smith, was just seven years old when her mother died suddenly. Her mother was young, just twenty-seven years old. "I don't remember dealing with it," Smith said.

> I was over [at] my friend's house across the street playing on the
> swings when we heard an ambulance and ran to see what was going

on . . . thinking it was exciting that there was an ambulance on our street. Then I saw them at my house and my friend's mother tried to hold me back from running over there. I just got to see [my mother] being put in the ambulance. She didn't see me. I don't know where my sisters were. Then my grandfather got us and brought us over his house next door and [had] us kneel down around a kitchen chair and pray. We were told she went to heaven with God. I thought she was coming back. I didn't understand it was forever.[5]

Today, at fifty-seven, Smith is still feeling the effects of this loss.

It's been fifty years. I have learned from that experience to just bury my feelings and not deal with anything that upsets me. In hindsight, I wish I had handled it all better, as things could've been quite different in the roads I chose throughout my life.[6]

Both Barbara Smith and Maureen O'Brien Smith think that talking about their parent would have helped them grieve. These two cousins suffered similar losses, but each family handled it differently. Each family unit is different, and the ways that families deal with grief differ from one family to the next. Maureen O'Brien Smith has the following advice for people going through this situation: "Talk about it, everything, that person, what happened—all of it."[7] For Barbara Smith, secrecy about what was going on made things worse:

Everyone was crying and felt sorry for us. . . . They were always whispering around us and it made me very mad. I wanted to yell at them all and tell them to shut up and stop talking about my mother, but I didn't. Family, the neighbors, the nuns at school. . . . It was very annoying. I felt like a total outsider.[8]

Human beings need to process their feelings and emotions. It is evident from the stories of these two women that the loss of a parent affects people well into their adulthood. It can affect the way people view relationships with their own children. It can create fear that the same thing will happen again. Maureen

For a child who has lost a parent, the regular celebrations of life—birthdays, graduations, holidays—are often bittersweet.

O'Brien Smith was afraid that she would die much like her mother had: "When I turned forty-one, my youngest was nine, so I was rather worried that whole year, like a nagging fear that it could happen to my kids."[9]

All Feelings Are Okay

Anger toward the parent who has died is not uncommon. Barbara Smith experienced some anger: "I did not think it was forever at first. Later, as I got a few years older, I got angry, almost blaming her [my mother] for leaving us."[10] Children can feel abandoned; then they may feel guilty for being angry at the deceased parent, and this cycle can continue on and on. It can help for children who lose a parent to talk to other children or teens going through the same thing. This way, they will know that some emotions are common among children left behind. They will be able to feel that they truly are talking to another person who really understands what they are going through and may find peace in that.

Children who have lost a parent can feel abandoned; then they may feel guilty for being angry at the deceased parent. This cycle can go on and on.

The surviving parent is suffering the loss of his or her spouse, though it is different from losing a parent. Being there for each other is important, but just as the surviving parent can benefit from talking about his or her emotions with other people who have lost a spouse, children who have lost a parent can be helped by talking to other children in the same situation. Every year, things will come up that stir up emotions—Mother's Day or Father's Day, birthdays, holidays, the anniversary of the parent's death. Having a support system in place can help children and teens get through these emotional times.

Mary Kukovich, who lost her mother to cancer when she

was fourteen, has some advice for teens going through the loss of a parent:

> Losing a parent is an awful thing at any age; someone once told me that no matter how old you are, your parents are like an umbrella over you. It's a real loss on so many levels, especially when you're young, and offering easy answers isn't what a teen wants to hear. I can say that the experience changes you profoundly, and if you're open to it, you can learn a great deal and grow from it. It may sound odd, but I think losing Mom as a teenager has made me a much better person today. I think that all of my brothers and sisters, as well as myself, tend to be more sensitive to other people, more accepting of differences, and more willing to try and make things work rather than arguing, because we saw early on that life is precious. It showed us how to put things in perspective, I think. My best advice would be to love the rest of your family openly and honestly, to try and understand what they're going through, to be willing to share your pain and be sensitive to theirs. Most of all, try to find peace in your heart—not an easy thing for anyone, let alone a teenager. It's also good to know that all around you, there are adults who share the wounds of losing a parent at a young age, and they can be real resources for you . . . not to offer advice, but to listen and cry with you. It might be a relative or a neighbor, a teacher or the parent of a friend. Try to find them. I wish I had.[11]

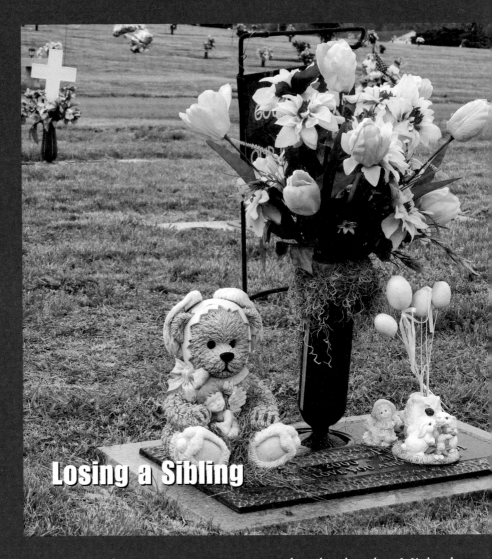

4 Losing a Sibling

Mary Ann O'Brien was twenty-seven when her brother Michael suddenly died at age twenty-one. They came from a large Irish family of eleven children. More than thirty years have passed since her brother died, but O'Brien still thinks of him often and tries to keep his memory alive. "I take every opportunity to speak about Mike, recalling all of the wonderful memories I have of him and of the good times we had together. The only advice I have is that with time the pain eases, your memories become so very important, and that person lives on in your heart."[1] Although O'Brien was an adult at the time her brother died, this demonstrates how strong the bond between siblings can be. Things, places, and people will sometimes trigger the memory of a sibling, and emotions can come rushing back many years later. For O'Brien, this proved true. "After thirty years, something will bring it all back. It will either bring tears to my eyes or a smile on my face."[2]

It can help for teens to share their feelings when a sibling has died. Not only is the teen suffering the loss of a brother or sister, he or she must also see the grief that other family members are going through during this time. Other siblings may not fully comprehend the situation. Often young children do not understand that death means the person is never coming back. They lack the ability to understand the finality of it. The parents who lost their child are experiencing an immense amount of pain. They have to console their surviving children while also dealing with their own grief.

People do not expect that they will bury their children. It goes against the natural order of things. So when people lose a child, it might be the single most devastating experience of their life. Parents who have suffered this loss may be in a state of shock and complete disbelief. When the shock subsides, intense sadness and grief can occur. Each member of the family is grieving in his or her own way. They are all trying to be there for other remaining family members while also dealing with the intense grief that they themselves are suffering. The family unit, at this point, is in crisis.

The Family Unit

The surviving siblings may feel awkward leaning on their parents for support when they see that their parents are in so much pain. Teens in crisis may then choose to bottle up their emotions because they don't want to further upset the already grieving parents and younger siblings. The family is a unit, a compilation of unique pieces, each member with his or her own place in the unit. After the death of a child, that unit is disrupted and feels incomplete. The unit that the family had come to know does not exist and will never exist again, because a piece of the puzzle is gone forever. A new family unit will emerge, one without the deceased sibling, and each person in the family must learn to function in this new unit. Families may not know how to function at first. They may need counseling as a family as well as individual counseling for each member of the family. To try to pretend that nothing has happened and go on with life as if nothing has changed can be harmful, especially to the surviving siblings, who may not fully understand what has occurred.

> **Surviving siblings may feel awkward leaning on their parents for support when they see that their parents are in so much pain.**

Marriages at Risk

The grief over the loss of a child is so strong that many marriages are not able to survive this crisis. Sometimes one spouse does not understand the coping mechanisms of the other spouse. One spouse might blame the other for the child's death or might have his or her own feelings of guilt. Sometimes anxiety or depression gets to be too much for the relationship to withstand. When a child dies, one spouse may like to talk about that child. She may feel that this is keeping the child's memory alive, which may be helping her with the healing process. The other spouse, however, may not be ready for this and may find it too painful to talk about the child. Neither spouse may understand the other's grieving process. "How can she want to talk about him all day and dig up all of these horrible feelings?" one might think. The other spouse may think, "How can he just forget about him so quickly?" Each person is devastated, but each is dealing with grief in his or her own unique way—and sometimes the inability to understand and communicate with each other about this grief can cause the marriage to fail.

Siblings are normally a constant presence in each other's lives. Adjusting to the loss of a brother or sister can be very difficult.

Feelings of Guilt

In most households, siblings are a constant presence in each other's lives, whether they get along or are constantly bickering. For children and teens, losing a sibling may mean that they feel uncertain about their own place in the family unit. The loss of the constant presence of their sibling is an adjustment that often proves difficult for those children left behind. Many young people who have lost siblings deal with feelings of guilt and regret.

Guilt is a big part of dealing with the death of a sibling. Brothers and sisters commonly bicker and fight. It is natural. When people live together, there are bound to be arguments—even more so if the people are siblings. Sometimes, siblings may think about how wonderful it would be to be an only child, doted on by both parents. Such wishes are usually fleeting and nothing more than an emotional response to a dispute with a sibling. When people lose a brother or sister and they think back to unkind thoughts they had or mean words they said, they may feel a tremendous amount of guilt. This feeling is normal, but sibling rivalry is normal, too.

It is important not to get caught up in a cycle of self-blame for arguing with the deceased sibling. Since members of the immediate family are grieving much like the teen is, it may be helpful to talk to a pastor, a counselor, an aunt or uncle, or another member of the extended family. Teens can begin to work through these feelings of guilt by talking about what they wish they had said or done when their sibling was still alive.[3] It is important for those working with children and teens who are grieving the loss of a sibling to understand that these feelings of guilt are very real. Some surviving siblings actually even feel a sense of guilt about the death itself, that in some way they caused it either by their actions or angry thoughts.[4] This is a tremendous burden to carry—and one that may impede further emotional growth if not worked through. If the surviving sibling's actions did contribute to the death in some way, then professional help would be a likely course due to the complex nature of the emotions involved in this type of situation.

Losing a Grandparent

Jim Kahlan was eighteen when his grandfather died at age seventy-three. For Kahlan, this was a very difficult time, as he and his grandfather had a very close relationship. Kahlan recalls:

> We had a very unique bond and we were always very close, and no matter what happened, he would always put a positive spin on things to make me feel better. At first I was upset. Then I became angry (especially at God for taking him) but after that I was just glad to have had him as a grandfather even though it was just for eighteen years. I wish it would have been a lot longer but I guess that is the way God works.[1]

It has been more than five years since Kahlan's grandfather

died, but even today this loss affects him. He often gets upset at the thought that his future children will never get to know this wonderful man.[2]

A Different Relationship

Grandparents often find a new youthfulness when a grandchild is welcomed into the family. They get to enjoy their grandchildren without stressing over parental issues. Barbara Smith lights up when she speaks about her five grandchildren (and one on the way). When asked about her relationship with them, she stated:

> I believe the bond between a grandparent and a grandchild is that of total, unconditional, one-on-one love. As a grandparent, we are not responsible to see that their homework is done, their room is clean, they brushed their teeth, and ate all their vegetables. That is their parents' responsibility. We don't have to nag them to do all the responsible things parents have to, so we are the good guys.[3]

Grandparents have raised their children, and now their children have children. Now their only job is to love their grandchildren. They get to play with them and have fun. They can just sit and watch these children grow up. Many feel they have earned this privilege, and they relish it.

> Grandparents often find a new youthfulness when a grandchild is welcomed into the family. They get to enjoy their grandchildren without stressing over parental issues.

A grandparent's home may be the one place where a child feels truly loved without judgment. Teens especially sometimes have conflicts of opinion with parents. The adolescent years can create some distance between parents and their teens as young people are often trying to figure out life and gain independence. However, these issues may not overlap into a teen's relationship with a grandparent, so this may feel like a very safe and loving relationship for the adolescent.

When the Grandparent Becomes a Parental Figure

Some children are raised by their grandparents. A grandparent may become the temporary guardian of children or teens if their mother or father is having difficulty managing the responsibilities of raising children along with the other stressors of life, such as work and paying bills. In other cases, the grandparent becomes the permanent guardian for his or her grandchildren. This could happen as a result of the death of a parent or abandonment by a parent. In this scenario, the grandparent is the parental figure and has the same duties of all other parents, including becoming the disciplinarian.

When a grandparent is raising a child or teenager, the two frequently forge a close relationship. The grandparent can be seen as a parental figure and also a fun person to spend time with. However, when a grandparent steps into the role of guardian for the adolescent, there may be some friction, because often teenagers are developing their own identity and may be rebellious. Now the fun-loving grandparent is put into the role of the enforcer, and the dynamic may shift. As a result, the relationship between grandparent and grandchild can become strained.

Losing a Grandparent

Because most grandparents are much older than their grandchildren, many teens may have to deal with the death of this member of their family. The death of a grandparent can be the first major loss they ever suffer. It may be sudden, following an event such as a heart attack, or it may be gradual, taking place after years of illness. When a grandparent dies suddenly and unexpectedly, grandchildren may go through periods of disbelief and denial. In other situations, grandchildren must learn to cope with the loss of a grandparent well before the grandparent dies, as in the case of long-term, debilitating illnesses.

Many grandparents enjoy their grandchildren because they can play with them and have fun rather than worrying about discipline and other parental issues.

Grief Before Death

Unfortunately, many older adults experience a decrease in their cognitive abilities as they progress through the years.[4] This is seen by many health professionals as a normal consequence of aging.[5] Older adults can experience memory problems, a decrease in the ability to recall information, and a decrease in the ability to process information. A grandparent may be experiencing some of these problems merely as the result of aging. However, for some grandparents, these can be signs of a more serious health condition.

One such condition is Alzheimer's disease, a very serious brain disorder. As of 2008, it affects some 5 million Americans.[6] Roughly 26.6 million people have Alzheimer's disease worldwide.[7] It is the most common type of dementia, or the loss of mental functions to a degree severe enough to interfere with daily functioning. With Alzheimer's disease, nerve cells in the brain die, and the signals that need to be transmitted through the brain for a person to function have difficulty completing transmission. As a result, memory, judgment, and thinking can become impaired. The decline in cognitive abilities of a grandparent may go unnoticed for a long time. Sometimes it is difficult for family members to discern when memory and thinking problems are just a part of aging and when they may indicate a serious condition such as Alzheimer's. It can, however, progress to the point where the grandparent is not able to recognize his or her own grandchild.

The debilitating nature of Alzheimer's disease and other physical and mental ailments that affect the elderly, such as cancer, heart disease, and stroke, can take years to develop. For families, it is often very difficult to watch a loved one's mind and body deteriorate. This can be especially hard for teens. Often teens may feel as though they have lost a grandparent long before the grandparent actually dies. With illnesses that affect cognition, it can feel as if the family no longer knows this person and that the person no longer knows his or her family members. With cancer and other debilitating diseases that attack the body, the grandparent may now look totally different. Sometimes people dying of an illness become depressed or moody. This is not a reflection of their feelings toward their grandchildren. They are grieving, too. They may know that the outlook is bleak. They may realize that they only have a very short time left and are grieving the time with their family they will never have. Good days and bad days should be expected, and bad days should not be taken personally. The entire family is in a state of crisis when a loved one is dying.

People can experience the grieving process well before the actual death of a loved one. They may be in denial that it is really happening. They may feel anger toward God for putting the family through this ordeal. They may yearn for a time when the dying person was healthy.

Many people are uncomfortable around someone who is very ill and thus distance themselves from the pain. It is hard for people to watch someone they love suffer. It is important to have a sounding board—someone to discuss feelings with. There are support groups just for grandchildren mourning the loss of a grandparent. Sometimes it helps to be with people who are going through a similar experience.

Losing a Friend

Richard Phillips was just sixteen when his friend Randy was killed while riding his motorcycle. Randy was just seventeen when he died. For Phillips, there was anger. He was angry at God, at the doctors, and also at Randy:

I was mad for a lot of reasons. The first one was that Randy was always pushing his dirt bikes, street bike and SUV to the limit. He never backed off. I can recall the only time I rode with him in a vehicle he was passing a car on a two-lane road while climbing a hill. We could not see the traffic over the crest of the hill, and he had no fear. Another reason why I was angry was that we were told he was going to be fine—that his injuries were not life-threatening and that he would be back on his feet in a few weeks. He died on the operating table of a blood clot. It pretty much stunned everyone. . . . The final reason I was angry was because he was one of the few people that I knew at that age that had a firm handle on what he wanted to do in life. His thinking was more of a seasoned veteran of life versus a kid who is not even out of high school. That is truly a waste; God took someone that would have made a difference in this world for the better.[1]

Teenagers often feel that they are indestructible. Many teens think, "That will never happen to me," but it can, especially if someone is fearless or reckless. Many teens suffer the death of a close friend in which the death is due to a traumatic event.

Automobile-Related Deaths

Motor vehicle accidents are the leading cause of death for fifteen- to twenty-year-olds in the United States.[2] Teens who have been drinking are less likely to wear seat belts, which contributes to the high fatality rate for teens involved in car accidents.[3] Many of these accidents are alcohol-related; in addition, some are due to the young driver being distracted or inexperienced. Many teen automobile deaths occur during prom and graduation celebrations, from April through June.[4]

According to these high statistics, many teens will experience the sudden and traumatic loss of a friend while in high school or college. Because friends and social groups are so important during the teenage years, this sudden loss can prove devastating for those friends left behind. Often teens do not know where to turn for help in dealing with these emotions. If it was an alcohol-related event, teens may feel angry at the friend who was killed or even angry at themselves, figuring that they could have done something to stop their friend from driving or from getting into a car with someone who had been drinking.

> Teenagers often feel that they are indestructible. Many teens think, "That will never happen to me."

Most teenagers are careful, responsible drivers. But being distracted or simply inexperienced contributes to the higher rate of accidents for this age group.

Drug and Alcohol Abuse

Drug use is another killer of teens in the United States. During the teen years, curiosity can peak. Unfortunately, for some this means experimenting with drugs and alcohol. Teenagers do not always understand the risks associated with drug and alcohol use. A teen may experiment with these things to satisfy curiosity, fit in, socialize, relieve boredom, relax, or relieve the pressures of life. Those at risk for drug and alcohol abuse include teens with a family history of drug and alcohol abuse, teens who are depressed or have low self-esteem, teens who feel like outcasts among their peers, and teens going through a traumatic event. Things to look for that may indicate that a teen is abusing drugs or alcohol are as follows:

School Violence

In recent years, many teens have lost friends through school violence, such as the shootings at Columbine High School in Littleton, Colorado, in 1999. Two students shot and killed a teacher and twelve students before taking their own lives.

In this situation, students experience an especially difficult loss. Some may have been wounded in the attack. Others were not hurt, but witnessed the violence and have to deal with that trauma as well. Most are mourning not one friend or teacher, but several. School violence of this type can take a very heavy toll on communities.

Emotional changes. Sudden mood swings, personality changes, paranoia, self-destructive behavior, irritability, demands for privacy, changes in appearance, worsening grades, giddy behavior, changes in friends, depression, apathy toward things once important to the teen, and poor decision making.

Physical changes. Red and glazed eyes with changes in pupil size, changes in appetite, changes in sleep patterns, poor coordination, shaky hands, blank stare, cough or runny nose, nausea, vomiting, sweating, smell of substance on person and clothes, needle marks, puffiness or paleness of the face, or hyperactivity.

Any of these can be an indication that something is wrong. It is important to be aware of these signs so that teens can notice a peer who may be in trouble. Many drug overdoses in teens are accidental and could have been avoided. That is why it is so important for teens to look out for each other. If someone suspects a friend to be abusing drugs and alcohol, it is important to talk to the friend and encourage him or her to get help. There are treatment facilities that specialize in helping teens. If the person denies that he or she has a problem, it might help to talk with a counselor who specializes in helping teens in order to get information and tips on how to approach this person again about the drug or alcohol abuse. Encouraging the teen to contact a professional may help get him or her on the road to recovery.

Teen Suicide

Not all drug-related deaths among teens are accidental. Some young people decide to take their own life. Suicide is the third leading cause of death for fifteen- to twenty-four-year-olds and the sixth leading cause of death for five- to fourteen-year-olds. This is a problem that needs to be addressed in the community, in schools, and in the home. It is important for parents, school personnel, and friends to know what signs to look for if they are concerned that a teen may be depressed or struggling to cope with the stressors of life. In 2005, nearly 55 percent of all gun-related deaths in the United States were suicides. Therefore, it is important for parents to make sure guns are not accessible to teens in the home.

Girls differ from boys when it comes to suicide. Data have indicated that girls think about suicide more than boys do and even attempt it twice as often as boys do by using drugs or cutting themselves. However, a boy is four times more likely to die as a result of suicide because boys tend to use more lethal methods such as guns or hanging.[5] Any time teens express a desire to take their own life, it should be taken seriously. It could be a cry for help, asking for someone to intervene and help them through this difficult time. No discussion of suicide should ever be taken lightly. It helps to be educated in what to look out for, as this will help people be able to identify behaviors in friends that might put them at risk.

Getting Help

One way to begin to help a friend in need is to talk to him or her. Many teens just want to be heard. Just letting a friend talk while listening without judgment may help him or her gather the strength to get through a difficult time. Be sure to tell

Suicide is the third leading cause of death among those aged 15–24.
Whenever someone expresses a desire to take his or her own life,
family and friends should take it seriously.

an adult or a mental health professional in order to get help immediately if a friend says that he or she wants to die or is thinking of suicide. When a person confides suicidal feelings in a friend, he or she is often calling out for help.

Not all teens will ask for help nor give any indication that they are suicidal. Sometimes a suicide comes as a complete shock. The family and friends of this person may then feel guilty, thinking that they missed something. They might blame themselves, thinking that had they only been more observant, this would not have happened. Sometimes a person is determined to take his or her own life, and there is nothing anyone can do to change that.

The death of a friend by suicide is extremely difficult to cope with, because in addition to the loss of a friend, there may be issues of anger and resentment toward the person who took his or her own life. The grieving family members and friends of a suicide victim may move through the different emotions of grief that most grieving people deal with; however, when a loved one has chosen to take his or her own life, this comes as a very traumatic shock. To compound this issue, the grieving people may feel as though they are being judged by others and may feel lonely and isolated.

No discussion of suicide should ever be taken lightly. It helps to be educated in what to look out for, as this will help people identify risky behaviors in friends.

Teens going through this loss may have a difficult time comprehending why their loved one has chosen to take this path and why he or she did not think about others when making this decision. Teens may be angry because they feel that the suicide was a way of getting back at them or hurting them for some reason. All of these emotions are normal reactions to such a traumatic event. That is why it is important for those grieving a loved one who has committed suicide to get support from peers in a similar situation. The anger and guilt can become overwhelming, especially for teens. Parents and family members of grieving teens need to be there for them, listen, and offer support. This is a very difficult time for them, and they need the love and support of family members and friends now more than ever.

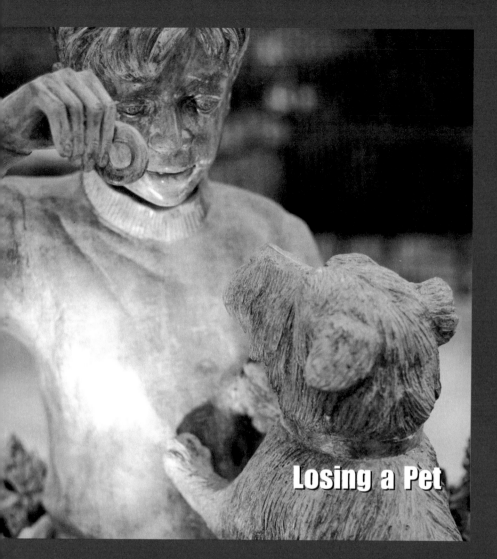

Losing a Pet

For many people, a pet is part of the family. Pets usually have short lives in comparison to humans, so most pet owners will experience the loss of a pet at some point. When a pet dies, it can often cause feelings of grief that were unexpected. For some, the loss of a pet may be harder to deal with than the loss of a relative. For those who don't have pets or have never owned a pet, grieving for a pet can seem silly. These people may trivialize the grief and treat it as if it is a joke. This can cause the pain the pet owner is already feeling to be increased because he or she is being told that these feelings of grief are silly or an overreaction. Margaret Phillips and her family had to make the decision

For many people, the relationship with a pet has all the attributes of a great friendship.

to euthanize their family dog, a German shepherd named Pita. Pita was loved by everyone in the family, and Phillips said, "Everyone was quite sad for a few months."[1] To those who don't understand why people grieve the loss of their pets, Phillips said, "I think that they have never experienced the love that a pet brings into one's life. It is the only true love you can buy."[2]

For many people, their relationship with their pet may have all of the attributes of a great friendship but without the conflicts that exist in human relationships. Pets offer companionship without judgment. To a pet owner, this animal may represent the purest of relationships. To have this relationship cut short can be very painful. As a result, the pet owner may have some of the same emotions and reactions discussed in earlier chapters, because he or she has in fact lost a loved one. Lack of concentration, disbelief, and extreme sadness can all be part of the process of grieving a pet.

Oprah Winfrey made the news in the summer of 2007 when Gracie, her two-year-old golden retriever, died suddenly. On May 26, 2007, Winfrey received news from one of her dog walkers that Gracie had choked on a plastic ball. Winfrey was shocked and devastated by the loss of her beloved animal. In her magazine, she remembered the upsetting event:

> **Pets usually have short lives in comparison to humans, so most pet owners will experience the loss of a pet at some point.**

> Gone??!! I couldn't believe what I was hearing. Yes, I saw it. I saw the caretaker rocking back and forth on the ground, his arms wrapped around himself, crying hysterically. My brain took in the whole scene, but it wasn't tracking properly. The first thing I remember saying is, "It's okay. It'll be okay. Tell me what happened." Through his sobs I heard: ". . . choked on a ball." And I knew, this was real. Gracie is gone, Gracie is gone, Gracie is gone kept repeating in my head.[3]

Through Gracie's death, Winfrey says, she received a message,

Some teenagers perceive a pet to be the only ally they have in the household.

as if she should take something away from this sad event. The message was: "Slow down, you're moving too fast."[4]

Different Ways to Lose a Pet

Pet loss can come in many different forms. The pet can die peacefully in its sleep from old age or die in an accident like Winfrey's Gracie. The circumstances may be different in these scenarios, but the outcome is the same. The pet is gone, and the grieving process begins. In some cases, the pet might have run away. Other times a family has to return the pet or give it away because it is just not working out. Whatever the circumstances, there is a sense of loss that may stir up many different emotions.

Guilt can be a big part of the grieving process for a pet. If a pet is suffering and has a poor quality of life, the pet owner has the option of euthanizing the pet—having it put to sleep by a veterinarian. Many pet owners do not make this decision lightly. Usually they have a number of conversations with a veterinarian about the pet's quality of life and the prognosis for the future. In some cases it may be more humane to euthanize the pet than to allow the pet to suffer. However, this decision can bring with it a lot of guilt. The pet owner did not let nature take its course. In this case, the pet owner had an active role in the ending of the pet's life, which can be difficult to accept.

When a Teenager Loses a Pet

When trying to gain independence, a teen sometimes has conflicts with parents and authority figures. This may cause tension between the teen and the rest of the family. Often a teen would much rather spend time with his or her social group than the family. Parents may not be able to understand why their teen no longer wants to spend time at home with the family and why the teen may be working so hard to detach from the family unit.

During this time, the family pet may be the only ally a teen has in the household. A pet does not care that the teen would rather spend Friday night with friends than playing Scrabble with the family. The pet does not care that the teen wants to be able to stay out until ten o'clock on school nights. As a result, a teen may feel closer to the family pet than to other members of the household.

After Saying Good-Bye

Grief for the loss of a pet is a real emotion. Here are some tips on dealing with the loss:

- Don't let people tell you that your feelings are silly or that you are overreacting to the loss of a pet. You are entitled to your feelings, and it is perfectly natural to be deeply saddened by the loss of a family pet.

- Talk about the pet with people you trust. It can help to express feelings of sadness for the loss of the pet. Keeping these feelings bottled up will only cause more sadness. It is okay to cry.

- Remember the good times with the pet.

- Avoid people who will minimize your feelings of grief for the pet.

- Consider joining a support group for people who have lost pets. There are groups in towns across the country that meet to discuss these issues. There are also online support groups for people grieving the loss of a pet.[5] These are good places to talk to people going through the same loss.

- If necessary, take some time before getting a new pet. People need to process their feelings of grief. If they do not, they may feel resentment toward the new pet. You need to be ready for a new pet to come into your life and your heart.

- When you do feel ready for a new pet, think carefully before choosing one similar to the previous pet. A new and healthy relationship with this new pet needs to be formed. For some people, this may be easier with a pet of a different breed or appearance.

Grieving pet owners should not allow others to belittle their feelings. They should utilize the same support systems that may be needed in the event of the death of a loved one or friend.

Last Will and Testament

Before and After Death

8

Many people dislike going to funerals and have no desire to plan one. When a friend or family member has died, it is a time of immense emotion and pain. The last thing many people want to do is plan a gathering, trying to keep track of details while in the midst of such intense emotions. During the days following a death, it may seem that the family and friends left behind are constantly making decisions. What kind of memorial service would he or she have wanted? Should it be private? Did he or she want to be buried or cremated?

Getting Affairs in Order

For people who have a terminal illness or people who just want to make sure that their family members are not left to figure out their wishes, there is a phrase that many use to describe getting everything taken care of so things are settled in the event of their death. It is called getting one's affairs in order. People know that it is not a good sign when they are told by their doctor to get their affairs in order. It means that death is a likely result of the illness or condition they are suffering from or that the illness or condition may cause mental impairment that will leave them no longer able to make decisions on their own.

Now they must make decisions about their finances, their medical care, any young children they may have, their property, and their wishes regarding a funeral or memorial service. With death, there are many details to deal with. Some people would rather avoid this topic entirely. People generally do not want to think about their death, their affairs, or their funeral. Some are even superstitious, thinking that if they plan for their death, they will die. However, it does help the immediate family left behind. When deceased people have previously made some decisions and gathered documentation that will be needed upon their death, this can lessen the burden on the family. If their wishes are clear and information is readily available, there will be less stress on the family, at least with regard to the planning process. Family members do not want to go on a wild goose chase for life insurance information and other related documents when a loved one has died. They are grieving; their concentration is poor. It is a difficult time, and it can be even more stressful if affairs were left in a state of disarray. When people are getting their affairs in order, decisions should be made about the following:

Finances. People should have a will in place and should make sure that it will accurately reflect their wishes. A will sets forth the deceased's wishes about assets and property.

People may also want to give someone power of attorney, the authorization to make financial decisions for them if and when they become incapacitated. This way they can rest assured, knowing that someone they trust will be making decisions for them if it becomes necessary.

Health care. It is a good idea for people to make their wishes known regarding their choices for their health care. They can achieve this by gathering documents known as advance directives. Do they want to be kept alive on a machine? What if they are not conscious—who will make decisions for them? They could sign a durable power of attorney for health care, which will state who will make decisions if they become incapacitated. They can feel comforted knowing that someone with their best interests at heart is making decisions when they are unable to.

Would they want to be resuscitated if their heart stops or they stop breathing? If not, they should sign a do-not-resuscitate (DNR) order, which will let those who are taking care of them know that they do not want to be revived or receive any other lifesaving treatment. When this order is in place, all medical personnel working with a patient are instructed that they cannot give CPR to the patient or otherwise try to resuscitate the person.

People may want to decide whether they would like to donate organs and tissue upon their death. Many lives are saved every year by donated organs. People can specify which organs they would like to donate, if any. Some states allow people to indicate when they receive their driver's license whether they want to be an organ donor. The license then reflects their wish to donate their organs upon their death.

What about pain management? People also might want to discuss what will happen should doctors give them a specific amount of time left to live. In that event, would they want hospice care? Hospice care is for people who have less than six

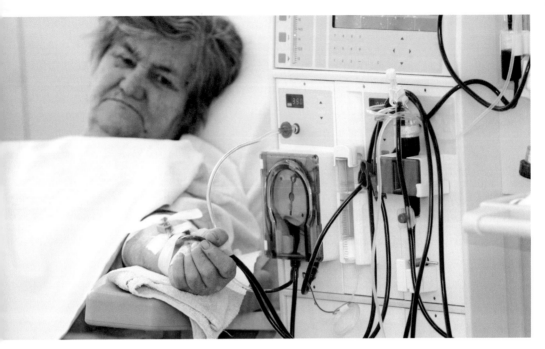

A durable power of attorney for health care is a document that specifies who will make medical decisions for someone. Above, a woman undergoes dialysis, a treatment for kidney disease.

months to live and wish to be as comfortable as possible during that time. It provides care with compassion for people in the last phases of an illness. The goal is not to treat the illness but rather to keep people comfortable by managing pain and minimizing suffering during their last months. Hospice programs also provide help to the dying person's family.

Making these decisions and getting affairs in order while one is still of sound mind and body will not only help the family members who are making plans and arrangements after death, it will also ensure that the deceased's wishes are respected.

Rituals

Once someone has died, a plan needs to be set in motion with regard to the disposal of the body and any memorial services planned for the person. It is time to say good-bye to the deceased.

Ritualistic farewells to the dead go back centuries. Every culture pays its respects to the dead in some fashion. Each culture has rituals in which people memorialize the dead while giving them a sacred place to rest for eternity, whether in the earth, above land, or scattered in the form of ashes. The rituals are often rooted in the prevalent religion of the culture. Some cultures believe that death is a new beginning into the beyond, while other cultures see death as the end to an existence and nothing else.

Today many cultures observe visitation, or visiting with the deceased. In Western societies, this usually takes the form of a wake at a funeral home, where the body is in either a closed or open casket. The term *wake* initially described a period of time when loved ones would watch the body of a person before it was buried, even during the nighttime hours. Some families use the time during a wake to share stories of the deceased. Often there are prayers offered for the deceased and the bereaved. Friends come to the funeral home to offer comfort to the family. There may be food and drink provided, as this is seen as a celebration of the person's life.

> **Every culture pays its respects to the dead in some fashion. The rituals are often rooted in the prevalent religion of the culture.**

In the Jewish religion, there are periods of mourning after the burial of the deceased. Shiva lasts one week from the date of the burial. During the first three days after the burial, members of the immediate family sit alone and mourn the loss of their loved one. During the last four days of shiva, friends and extended family can visit the immediate family, bringing food with them. After shiva, the next period is called sheloshim, which lasts for thirty days after the burial. During this time, the family can resume daily activities, though they continue to mourn, and they may continue to recite the Kaddish prayer every day. After sheloshim, the prayer is recited every Sabbath in the person's honor for twelve months. At this time, close family and friends also visit the gravesite where the grave monument is unveiled. After twelve months, mourning is over except for brief moments on the anniversary of the death, Yarhzeit (according to the Hebrew calendar).

Rituals are ways for people to stay connected to their culture or faith during a time of mourning. Each culture has its own set of rituals, but some rituals transcend many cultures. The ritual of wearing black when mourning has been utilized in many cultures. It garnered a lot of attention during the nineteenth century in Europe and the United States, when widows were expected to dress exclusively in black for the first year; during the second, they could add a bit of black jewelry to their ensemble. During the last six months of mourning, they could introduce colors such as violet, gray, and white.

Burials and Memorials

Upon death, a body can be buried, cremated, or donated for scientific research. The deceased's body can be buried in a casket in the ground or in a mausoleum above ground. Bodies can also be cremated and the ashes buried, kept in an urn on display, or scattered over land or sea, often in an area that was special to the deceased. Burial arrangements can be made before death by the person involved or afterward by the person's family.

Shortly after the death, the person's family usually writes an obituary that will be submitted to the local newspaper, informing the public of the death and also of the life of their loved one. Sometimes, especially for famous people, obituaries are written ahead of time and kept on file, to be updated at the time of death.

In addition to deciding on the disposition of the body and

A U.S. flag is folded over the casket of a soldier. Certain traditions and rituals are followed for military funerals.

what to say in an obituary, family and friends must decide on the type of memorial that would best suit the deceased. If the deceased was part of this discussion prior to his or her death, these decisions are easier to make.

Each culture has its own traditions and customs with regard to funeral services. Some cultures promote the use of a eulogy, or a tribute to the deceased's life. It is often given by someone who was close to the person. Since people may have a hard time reading a eulogy because they are still raw with emotion, it is not uncommon for a person close to the deceased to write the eulogy, which someone else who is less emotional then reads to the people attending the service.

In Orthodox Jewish and Muslim traditions, the funeral and burial are supposed to take place as soon as possible after death, usually within a day; cremation is forbidden. In Christian churches, practices are more variable.

In some traditions, flowers are sent by family and friends to the funeral home, the church, or the person's home. Often flowers are placed on the grave on special days following the death, such as holidays and the person's birthday. Among Jews, people visiting the grave place a small stone upon it to show they have been there and to honor the dead person.

A memorial service differs from a funeral in that the body is not present, and it can be held some time after the death.

Picking Up the Pieces

After the funeral services and visitors, life will go back to normal in the sense that people will return to their daily activities. Children and teens will go back to school, adults will go back to work, and life and all of its responsibilities will resume. It will now be time for those left behind to adapt to this new life without their loved one.

In the days, weeks, and months after a death, there comes a time when the family will need to decide what to do with the belongings of the deceased. This may be too painful to face right away, so this can even occur even years after the death. If the deceased is a child, did the child have his or her own room? If so, what will happen to that room? Should the room be kept as it was when the child was alive? Should the clothes and toys be donated to charity or should the family keep them because of the memories associated with them? These are all difficult decisions that should not be made in haste. In the case of the death of an immediate family member, the family may want to discuss this as a group so everyone has input into the decision. One member may feel that holding on to these items is like holding on to the pain; for this person, the items must be disposed of in some way so the family can move on. Another member of the family may fear that memories of this person will fade if they dispose of the belongings. This is a very difficult decision for people to make, and each family has to make the best decision for the family as a whole.

> There comes a time when the family will need to decide what to do with the belongings of the deceased. This may be too painful to face right away, so this can occur even years after the death.

Some people who are grieving may also have unfinished business with the deceased. Maybe they have feelings of guilt for something said or something not said. Maybe they are seeking a way to channel some of their grief into an activity that helps them. There are many ways that people who are grieving can stay connected to the deceased while still working through their grief process.

Writing. Writing can be an effective tool for people who are dealing with grief. It may help take some of the burden off of people who are mourning if they write a letter to the loved one or friend saying the things that they wished they had said when the person was alive.

Journaling can also be very helpful. People can write down

their feelings and be sure that they will not be judged on their thoughts. A journal is a place where people can feel safe pouring out their heart on paper. It can be a very cathartic experience for those grieving a loved one or friend.

Art. Creating a photo album, memory book, or collage in tribute to the person who has died can be helpful for many people. Such art can include stories about the person and things that made that person special. Today many younger people create Web sites in honor of their lost loved ones or friends. This way others can visit the site and feel a sense of comfort knowing that the person is not forgotten.

A middle schooler looks at a display of quilts made in memory of people who died of AIDS. Creating art to memorialize a loved one can be a meaningful part of the grief process.

For younger children, a memory bear may be something that will help provide comfort. This is a teddy bear made out of something that once belonged to the deceased, such as clothes or a favorite blanket. It allows the child to feel close to the person. Some children and adults are comforted by quilts made from the clothing of their loved one.

Growth. Some people opt to plant a tree in honor of the deceased. They watch the tree grow year after year, which helps them feel that the spirit of the person lives on.

Giving. Some people enjoy participating in events that benefit certain charities or organizations. If the loved one or friend has died from an illness for which research funds are being raised, people may want to raise funds for the group by participating in charity races or other events. They are able to meet others affected by the illness and also to feel as though they are doing something to help fight the illness or condition.

Often people donate money in honor of the deceased. Sometimes information on such gifts is part of the obituary, specifying that donations be made to a hospice, a scholarship fund, disease research, or some other recipient in lieu of, or instead of, flowers.

Giving Comfort

Sometimes when people are trying to comfort someone who is grieving, they find themselves at a loss for words. Other times they are not at a loss for words at all—but they don't have the right words. People who are grieving are not helped by hearing things like "You can always remarry" or "You are still young, you can have another child." If you don't know what to say, just say that you are so sorry for their loss. Saying something simple is better than saying something inappropriate.

In her book *How Can I Help: How to Support Someone Who Is Grieving,* June Cerza Kolf warns against using clichés. She offers some suggestions on phrases to avoid and more appropriate responses to use instead:

What Not to Say	*What to Say Instead*
Time heals everything.	You must feel as if this pain will never end.
Try to look for the good in this situation.	This is just too painful to bear.
Your loved one is better off.	Your loved one is no longer suffering, but I know you certainly are.
The Lord never gives us more than we can handle.	This must be so very hard for you.
Try not to cry.	It is okay to cry. Cry as much as you need to.
I know just how you feel.	I can't even imagine how you must feel. Just know how much I care.
Everything will be okay.	Please let me help however I can.
Let me know if I can do anything.	I'll call tomorrow to see how I can help.[1]

Both before and after death, there are ways for the family and friends of those who are grieving to help. They can help out by getting affairs in order, offering support, and just letting their loved ones know that they are available and ready to listen and help at any time.

Support for One Another

9

Lacey was seven years old when her father was murdered. He was shot and later died at the hospital. Since she was the youngest of the three children, Lacey was not allowed to go to the hospital with her brother and sister.

> I wasn't able to go to the hospital with him, which really hurt because my brother and sister were able to. But everyone felt I was too young, so I was sent to a relative. I guess I just assumed that he would be home soon. I never thought that would be it. I guess I was confused, mainly. I just couldn't seem to understand that that was it. No *good-bye*s, no *I love you*s, and no more *good night*s.[1]

For Lacey, this tragedy erased any memory of her childhood

before that point. She said, "My father's death wiped out all of my memories before then. I know it seems strange, but believe me—I would love to remember being a kid, but I just can't seem to."[2] Having gone through such a traumatic event, Lacey understands the importance of relying on friends and family for support at such a difficult time. "Lean on your family and friends," she said. "Never keep it bottled in. Talk to someone; just reach out, even if you just want a shoulder to cry on. The battle that we fight within ourselves to remain strong is the hardest that we will ever have to deal with."[3]

Responses to Grief

Some people may learn to get past the grief eventually, but for others the death of a loved one has changed their lives forever. The person who has died was a part of them in life, and many people want to keep it that way even after the death. People who are grieving experience many reactions, some expected and some unexpected. Knowing that some reactions are common may be helpful for people who are in the process of grieving.

Since the body and mind are interconnected, there are physical, behavioral, mental, spiritual, and emotional reactions associated with grief. It is important to be aware of these changes so people can recognize them in loved ones and friends but also in themselves. Mary Ann Emswiler and James Emswiler, in their book *Guiding Your Child Through Grief*, compiled the following list of reactions that younger people may experience in response to death:

Emotional Reactions
- Crying, weepiness
- Hiding grief
- Being easily startled
- Loneliness

Behavioral Reactions

- Sexually acting out
- Risky behavior
- Restlessness
- Withdrawal
- Clingy behavior, not wanting to be alone
- Regression back to habits of younger years
- Reacting to stress
- Less productive in schoolwork
- Avoiding reminders of the person who died

Mental Reactions

- Problems with concentration
- Boredom
- Absentmindedness
- Lack of interest in hobbies or school

Spiritual Reactions

- Dreams and paranormal experiences during which the person dreams of the deceased person or feels his or her presence

Physical Reactions

- Change in appetite
- Fatigue
- Physical complaints and physical weakness
- Headaches
- Stomachaches
- Change in sleeping habits[4]

Many of these are normal reactions to grief. However, family members and friends must continue to observe the grieving person to see if any of these reactions seem to be more severe. For

Someone who is grieving may withdraw from friends, not wanting to participate in usual activities or hang out with the usual crowd.

example, has the weepiness and sadness turned into suicidal thoughts? Has a tendency for the person to withdraw turned into complete isolation? Has the person turned to drugs and alcohol to feel better? Often grieving people feel like they are the only person on earth going through such pain. They may look around and see people going about their everyday lives, eating dinner, playing ball, and catching the bus, and they may wonder, "Why am I the only person who feels so incredibly sad?" or "Do these people have any idea how terrible I feel right now? No! They are smiling and having fun while I feel absolutely awful inside." This type of thinking can sink people further and further into despair.

How Can People Help?

Here are some things people can do to help friends or family members during this difficult time:

Listening. If grieving people want to talk about the deceased person, then share a story about the person they are grieving if possible. It can be a funny story or just something silly the person used to do. If they would rather discuss other subjects, let them. Whether it is about sports, their feelings, or school, talk with them about whatever seems to help at the moment. Listening can be an effective tool in helping someone who is grieving.

Accepting. Understand that grieving people have suffered a loss that might change them in some ways forever. People learn to live with loss but may be a little different from then on, as a piece of them is now missing. Accept them even if they are changed in some ways forever.

Don't take any declined invitation as a rejection. Friends or family members who are grieving may not be ready to go out and enjoy the same things they used to, at least not right away. Don't take it personally. People move back into day-to-day activities at their own pace. Give them space if they need it. Be

One of the best ways to help a person who is grieving is just to be available to listen.

attentive to their needs. If they desire company and support, be sure to continue to act as you have always acted; if you usually call them every day, continue to do so if they are open to that. If they are not up to speaking, most likely they will let you know. Don't avoid a grieving person because it feels awkward.

Writing. Send your friend a note expressing your condolences, or write a letter or poem about the person he or she is grieving. Or buy a card that expresses how you feel. Many bereaved people save such notes and find comfort in them long after they are sent.

Helping. Offer to help out with chores around the house, errands, or anything your friend might need a hand with. During a time of grief, it can be difficult for a person to keep up with day-to-day tasks that need to be taken care of.

How Grieving People Can Help Themselves

When people are grieving, especially if this is the first time they have lost a loved one or friend, some emotions, experiences, and reactions from others might be unexpected and, as a result, invoke more emotion. It might help to know that certain situations can trigger emotional reactions. Understanding that there will be good days and bad days is important. Important dates such as birthdays and holidays may be difficult, and that is okay. If an important person is gone, it is normal to feel that loss even for years to come. For some people, holidays and momentous events trigger sadness. For others, it is the period leading up to the event that triggers strong emotion. For Corinne Hanson, who lost her husband, the days before an event sometimes proved to be the hardest. Hanson said:

> I found the days themselves less difficult than I thought because I'd been so worried about getting through them. Often the time leading up to the important day is more difficult—I'd think, "Why am I so depressed?" and then realize I was coming up on my husband's birthday.[5]

With the sadness and pain that some people experience as the result of the death of a loved one or friend, they may be tempted to self-medicate. Grieving people should avoid the temptation to use drugs or alcohol to numb pain. This may only cause more problems. It is also important for people not to forget to take care of themselves physically. They should try to get enough rest, eat well, and take care of their body. This can become difficult because eating and sleeping habits often change during a time of immense grief. However, when the body begins to break down and become weak, this can exacerbate any emotional issues the person is already going through at the time.

It is okay to express emotions. If a grieving person is angry, that is okay. If he or she is crying, that is okay, and if he or she is not crying, that is okay too. Just because others are handling loss in a certain way doesn't mean that everyone has to be having the same responses. Each person grieves in his or her own way and at different times.

Many people grieving the loss of a loved one are devastated. Sometimes they need help working through these emotions but are fearful that others will think they are crazy if they seek the help of outside resources. Grieving is just one of the many reasons a person can seek the help of mental health professionals and support services. It does not mean that the person is crazy or mentally ill; it just means that he or she is looking for support during this time of grief and pain.

Grief Therapy and Grief Counseling

In his book *Grief Counseling and Grief Therapy: A Handbook for the Mental Health Professional,* J. William Worden, Ph.D., distinguishes between grief therapy and grief counseling. He reserves grief therapy for situations in which there is an abnormal or complicated grief reaction.[6] Grief counseling, he states, helps people with uncomplicated normal grief.[7] If

Grief counseling is often conducted in a group setting. People can find it very helpful to talk with others who have also lost a loved one.

someone seems to be suffering from complicated grief, therapy with a professional may be warranted.

There are some things that distinguish grief therapy from grief counseling.

Grief therapy is generally more structured, often done in a one-on-one setting, and led by a trained professional in the field of grief and bereavement.[8] Grief counseling, on the other hand, is less structured, is done in a group setting or private setting, and can be facilitated by someone without specific training in grief and bereavement.[9] The intensity and duration of a person's reactions will determine whether there is a need for grief counseling or grief therapy.

Where to Find Support

Teenagers who are grieving have the same needs as adults.[10] However, many teens do not like to stand out.[11] Because teens feel comfortable around other teens, one place that may be comforting is a local support group for teens dealing with the loss of a loved one. Peers can look to each other for support. Although the loss may be different for each teen, the other issues involved with being a teenager are the same. It may help to talk with people of the same age and in the same community who are going through the same thing.

Contacting the local mental health association to see if it could provide a list of groups in the area is a good place to start. Teens can also look online. Many places that offer support counseling have Web sites. There are also Web-based support groups, in which people communicate strictly online. This type of support system may help some people, but others may need the physical support from the group, such as hugs and activities done during the group meetings that help with grief. Also, religious organizations, local hospitals, and facilities that provide hospice care may have a list of counseling support groups in the area.

Students pray together following a school shooting in Jacksboro, Tennessee. Often teens find it helpful to be in support groups with others who have gone through the same experience.

The teen might also want to set up an appointment with a private grief therapist for a one-on-one session. This type of talk therapy can be very helpful for people going through a crisis. Be sure to specify the need to speak with a bereavement therapist—someone skilled and trained specifically in providing therapy to those who are grieving and those who may be having complicated grief reactions.

> Seeking the help of mental health professionals does not mean that a person is mentally ill; it just means that he or she is looking for support during this time of grief and pain.

People can also go to their church and speak with a member of the clergy about their feelings. When someone dies, people sometimes get angry at God or have questions about their faith. Talking to a clergyperson can help those who are looking for spiritual guidance.

The Road Ahead

Working through grief emotions can be very difficult. For many people, the grief will subside but the loss will be with them forever. Understanding the emotions involved in the grief process and discussing how life changes as the result of the death of a loved one are important in understanding the journey ahead. For many people, the death of a loved one is one of the most difficult times in their lives. But with the support of friends, family, and professionals, they will get through it.

Sigmund Freud, a pioneer in the field of psychiatry, described how feelings of grief may subside over time but how the loss can become a part of the grieving person. In a letter dated April 12, 1929, to his friend and colleague Ludwig Binswanger, Freud wrote about the feelings he experienced after the death of his daughter, Sophie. Sophie would have been thirty-six on the day the letter was written. She had died in 1920, at twenty-six years of age, from complications related to the Spanish flu. In his letter to his friend, Freud wrote:

Although we know that after such a loss the acute state of mourning will subside, we also know we shall remain inconsolable and will never find a substitute. No matter what may fill the gap, even if it be filled completely, it nevertheless remains something else. And actually this is how it should be. It is the only way of perpetuating that love which we do not want to relinquish.[12]

Grieving is over when a person can reinvest their emotions into life and in the living.[13] At some point, many people who are left behind stop grieving, but they will never stop missing their loved one. They will merely learn to live with the memories of times shared with that person.

Chapter Notes

Chapter 1 Death Is a Part of Life

1. Julie Smith, personal interview, July 3, 2007.

2. Ibid.

3. Ibid.

4. Ibid.

5. Dan Schaeffer and Christine Lyons, *How Do We Tell the Children? A Step-by-Step Guide for Helping Children Cope When Someone Dies* (New York: Newmarket Press, 2001), p. 99.

6. Alan D. Wolfelt, *Understanding Grief: Helping Yourself Heal* (New York: Routledge, 1992), p. 138.

Chapter 2 The Grieving Process

1. J. William Worden, *Grief Counseling and Grief Therapy: A Handbook for the Mental Health Professional*, third edition (New York: Springer Publishing Company, 2001), p. 25.

2. Brook Noel and Pamela D.Blair, *I Wasn't Ready to Say Goodbye: Surviving, Coping, and Healing After the Sudden Death of a Loved One* (Naperville, Ill.: Sourcebooks, Inc., 2008), p. 28.

3. "'Megan's Law' Killer Escapes Death Under N.J. Execution Ban," *CNN.com*, December 17, 2007, <http://www.cnn.com/2007/POLITICS/12/17/death.penalty/index.html> (June 18, 2008).

4. Mary Kukovich, personal interview, August 1, 2007.

5. "How to Deal with Grief," National Mental Health Information Center, <http://mentalhealth.samhsa.gov/publications/allpubs/Ken-01-0104/default.asp> (June 18, 2008).

6. Mary Kukovich, personal interview, August 1, 2007.

7. Worden, p. 27.

8. Corinne Hanson, personal interview, March 28, 2008.

9. Worden, p. 32.

10. Ibid., p. 37.

11. Alan D. Wolfelt, *Understanding Grief: Helping Yourself Heal* (New York: Routledge, 1992), pp. 135–142.

12. Paul K. Maciejewski, Baohui Zhang, Susan Block and Holly Prigerson, "An Empirical Examination of the Stage Theory of Grief," *The Journal of the American Medical Association*, vol. 297, no. 7, February 21, 2007.

13. Ibid.

14. Worden, p. 10.

15. Ibid.

16. Ibid., p. 12.

17. William C. Kroen, *Helping Children Cope With the Loss of a Loved One* (Minneapolis: Free Spirit Publishing, Inc., 1996), p. 25.

Chapter 3 Losing a Parent

1. Maureen O'Brien Smith, personal interview, July 31, 2007.

2. Ibid.

3. Brook Noel and Pamela D. Blair, *I Wasn't Ready to Say Goodbye: Surviving, Coping, and Healing After the Sudden Death of a Loved One* (Naperville, Ill.: Sourcebooks, Inc., 2008), p. 157.

4. Maureen O'Brien Smith, personal interview, July 31, 2007.

5. Barbara Smith, personal interview, July 31, 2007.

6. Ibid.

7. Maureen O'Brien Smith, personal interview, July 31, 2007.

8. Barbara Smith, personal interview, July 31, 2007.

9. Maureen O'Brien Smith, personal interview, July 31, 2007.

10. Barbara Smith, personal interview, July 31, 2007.

11. Mary Kukovich, personal interview, August 1, 2007.

Chapter 4 Losing a Sibling

1. Mary Ann O'Brien, personal interview, July 31, 2007.

2. Ibid.

3. Barbara D Rosof, *The Worst Loss: How Families Heal from the Death of a Child* (New York: Henry Holt and Company, 1994), p. 33.

4. Ibid., p. 32.

Chapter 5 Losing a Grandparent

1. Jim Kahlan, personal interview, July 31, 2007.

2. Ibid.

3. Barbara Smith, personal interview, July 31, 2007.

4. "Guidelines for the Evaluation of Dementia and Age-Related Cognitive Decline," American Psychological Association, Presidential Task Force on the Assessment of Age-Consistent Memory Decline and Dementia, February 1998, <http://www.apa.org/practice/dementia.html> (July 29, 2007).

5. "Age Associated Memory Impairment," NYU Medical Center/NYU School of Medicine Alzheimer's Disease Center, n.d., <http://www.med.nyu.edu/adc/forpatients/memory.html> (July 29, 2007).

6. "What Is Alzheimer's," Alzheimer's Association, n.d., <http://www.alz.org/alzheimers_disease_what_is_alzheimers.asp> (July 29, 2007).

7. "100 Million Worldwide May Have Alzheimer's by 2050," *Forbes.com*, June 10, 2007, <http://www.forbes.com/forbeslife/health/feeds/hscout/2007/06/10/hscout605273.html> (July 29, 2007).

Chapter 6 Losing a Friend

1. Richard Phillips, personal interview, August 1, 2007.

2. "Traffic Crashes Are the Number One Killer of Teens—Nearly One-Third Are Alcohol-Related," National Highway Safety Traffic Administration, n.d., <http://www.nhtsa.dot.gov/people/injury/alcohol/Stopimpaired/planners/2311_ParentYouthPlanner/images/downloads/ParentsTeensFS.pdf > (June 18, 2008).

3. Ibid.

4. Tammy LaGorce, "Confronting Prom Night Drinking," *The New*

York Times, June 1, 2008, <http://www.nytimes.com/2008/06/01/nyregion/nyregionspecial2/01Rproms.html> (June 18, 2008).

5. "Suicide in the U.S.: Statistics and Prevention," National Institute of Mental Health, n.d., <http://www.nimh.nih.gov/health/publications/suicide-in-the-us-statistics-and-prevention.shtml> (June 18, 2008).

Chapter 7 Losing a Pet

1. Margaret Phillips, personal interview, June 14, 2008.

2. Ibid.

3. "What I Know for Sure," *O, The Oprah Magazine*, August 2007, <http://www.oprah.com/omagazine/200708/omag_200708_mission.jhtml> (July 29, 2007).

4. Ibid.

5. See, for example, *Petloss.com*, <http://petloss.com> (July 29, 2007).

Chapter 8 Before and After Death

1. June Cerza Kolk, *How Can I Help: How to Support Someone Who Is Grieving* (Cambridge, Mass.: DaCapo Press, 1991), pp. 11–12.

Chapter 9 Support for One Another

1. Lacey [last name withheld], personal interview, August 1, 2007.

2. Ibid.

3. Ibid.

4. Mary Ann Emswiler and James P. Emswiler, *Guiding Your Child Through Grief* (New York: Bantam Books, 2000), p. 38.

5. Corinne Hanson, personal interview, March 28, 2008.

6. J. William Worden, *Grief Counseling and Grief Therapy: A Handbook for the Mental Health Professional*, third edition (New York: Springer Publishing Company, 2001), p. 51.

7. Ibid.

8. Brook Noel and Pamela D. Blair, *I Wasn't Ready to Say Goodbye:*

Surviving, Coping, and Healing After the Sudden Death of a Loved One (Naperville, Ill.: Sourcebooks, Inc., 2008), pp. 220–221.

  9. Ibid.

10. June Cerza Kolk, *How Can I Help: How to Support Someone Who Is Grieving* (Cambridge: DaCapo Press, 1991), p. 26.

11. Ibid.

12. Sigmund Freud, *Letters of Sigmund Freud,* reprint edition (Mineola, New York: Dover Publications, 1992), p. 386.

13. Worden, p. 46.

Glossary

advance directive—Legal documentation stating the care and treatment that a person will receive should he or she become unable to make decisions affecting his or her health.

Alzheimer's disease—A progressive neurological disease of the brain that leads to dementia.

apathy—A lack of interest or concern or a lack of emotion or feeling.

bereavement—A state of sadness, mourning, and grief after a loved one has died.

bickering—Fighting about insignificant things.

burial—The ritual of placing a corpse in a grave.

cognition—Mental processing that involves awareness, perception, reasoning, and judgment.

cremation—The process of incinerating a dead body.

dementia—Deterioration of intellectual faculties, such as memory, concentration, and judgment, resulting from an organic disease or a disorder of the brain.

depression—An illness involving both the body and mind in which a person has changes in eating and sleeping habits as well as concentration. A person may feel sad and have a loss of interest in activities once enjoyed.

despair—Loss of hope.

diabetes—A disease in which the body does not properly control the sugar levels in a person's blood.

Do Not Resuscitate order (DNR)—Instructions ordering medical personnel not to administer life-sustaining treatment on a person.

durable power of attorney for health care—A written advance directive in which a person names an agent who will make decisions regarding health care and treatment in the event that the patient cannot make his or her own decisions.

euthanize—To end a life in the most painless way possible.

guilt—Remorse caused by a feeling that one has done something wrong.

hospice—A facility that provides special care for people who have less than six months to live, where a focus is placed on comfort, not treatment.

Kaddish—A prayer recited in daily synagogue services and by Jewish mourners after the death of a close relative.

magical thinking—Nonscientific reasoning that includes such ideas as connections between unrelated events and the mind's ability to affect the physical world.

mausoleum—A large burial chamber that is usually above ground.

paranoia—Distrust of others and things that is not based on rational thought.

power of attorney—The legal authority to act on another's behalf.

sheloshim—Including the seven days of shiva, this is the thirty-day period after the burial of a family member in the Jewish faith.

shiva—Mourning period, in the Jewish faith, of seven days after the death of a close relative.

will—A legal document that declares the wishes of a deceased person with regard to their assets.

yahrzeit—In the Jewish faith, the anniversary of the death of a relative .

yearning—Deep longing.

For More Information

American Association of Suicidology
4201 Connecticut Avenue, NW
Suite 408
Washington, DC 20008
202-237-2280

American Trauma Society
8903 Presidential Parkway
Suite 512
Upper Marlboro, MD 20772
800-556-7890

Compassionate Friends, Inc., National Headquarters
P.O. Box 3696
Chicago, IL 60522-3696
877-969-0010

Kids in Crisis
1 Salem Street
Cos Cob, CT 06807
203-622-6556

Motherless Daughters
P.O. Box 663
Prince Street Station
New York, NY 10012
212-614-8041

National Hospice Organization
1700 Diagonal Road, Suite 625
Alexandria, VA 22314
800-646-6460

Survivors of Suicide

Suicide Prevention Center
184 Salem Avenue
Dayton, OH 45406
513-223-9096

Teen Age Grief, Inc.

P.O. Box 220034
Newhall, CA 91322-0034
661-253-1932

Youth Suicide National Center

1825 Eye Street, NW
Suite 400
Washington, DC 200006
202-429-2016

Further Reading

Dennison, Amy, Allie, and David. *After You Lose Someone You Love: Advice and Insight from the Diaries of Three Kids Who've Been There.* Minneapolis: Free Spirit Publishing, 2005.

Goldberg, Neal C., and Miriam Liebermann. *Saying Goodbye: A Handbook for Teens Dealing With Loss and Mourning.* Southfield, Mich.: Targum Press, 2004.

Gootman, Marilyn E. *When a Friend Dies: A Book for Teens About Grieving and Healing.* Minneapolis: Free Spirit Publishing, 2005.

Hughes, Lynn B. *You Are Not Alone: Teens Talk About Life After the Loss of a Parent.* New York: Scholastic Paperbacks, 2005.

Norman, Liane Ellison. *The Duration of Grief.* Pittsburgh: Smoke and Mirror Press, 2005.

Thornhill, Jan. *I Found a Dead Bird: The Kid's Guide to the Cycle of Life and Death.* Toronto: Maple Tree Press, 2006.

Wray, T. J., with Ann Back Price. *Grief Dreams: How They Help Heal Us After the Death of a Loved One.* San Francisco: Jossey-Bass, 2005.

Internet Addresses

Association for Pet Loss and Bereavement
<http://www.aplb.org>

Fernside: Supporting children and families through grief
<http://www.fernside.org>

GriefNet.org: An Internet community of persons dealing
with grief, death, and major loss
<http://www.griefnet.org>

Yellow Ribbon Suicide Prevention Program
<http://www.yellowribbon.org>

Index